S0-AEB-157

THE SUN & MOON SIGNS LIBRARY

LIBRA

SEPTEMBER 23 – OCTOBER 23

JULIA AND DEREK PARKER

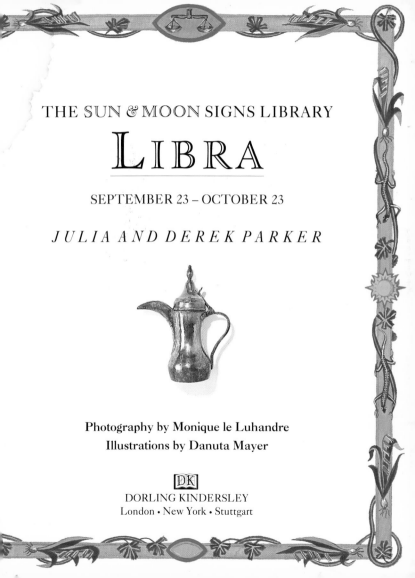

Photography by Monique le Luhandre
Illustrations by Danuta Mayer

DK

DORLING KINDERSLEY
London • New York • Stuttgart

Dedicated to James Ferguson

DK

A DORLING KINDERSLEY BOOK

Editor **Tom Fraser**
Art Editor **Ursula Dawson**
Managing Editor **Krystyna Mayer**
Managing Art Editor **Derek Coombes**
Production **Antony Heller**
U.S. Editor **Laaren Brown**

Computer page make-up Patrizio Semproni.
Photography p 11 © Michael Holford/British Museum;
p 16 Tim Ridley. Stylist pp 28-29 Lucy Elworthy. Illustration
pp 60-61 Kuo Kang Chen. Jacket illustration Peter Lawman.
With thanks to Carolyn Lancaster and John Filbey.

First American Edition, 1992
10 9 8 7 6 5 4 3 2 1

Published in the United States by
Dorling Kindersley, Inc., 232 Madison Avenue
New York, N.Y. 10016

Library of Congress Catalog Card Number 92-52790
ISBN 1-56458-090-3

Reproduced by GRB Editrice, Verona, Italy
Printed and bound in Hong Kong by Imago

CONTENTS

INTRODUCING
LIBRA

LIBRA, THE SIGN OF THE SCALES, IS THE SEVENTH SIGN OF THE
ZODIAC. LIBRANS NEED HARMONY AND BALANCE IN THEIR
LIVES. THE RULING PLANET OF THE SIGN IS VENUS, NAMED AFTER
THE GODDESS OF LOVE – AND TO LIBRANS, LOVE IS ALL.

Peace is important to Librans, and
they will sometimes try to obtain
it at any price. Although they often
have a reputation for laziness, it is
generally undeserved. They usually
have the motivation to work hard, but
always make time to listen to others.
Decision-making is hard for them as
they always see both sides of a
problem and tend to procrastinate.

Librans must be careful not to be
overindulgent, since this may lead to
weight gain that will spoil their
natural good looks.

Traditional groupings

As you read through this book you
will come across references to the
elements and the qualities, and to
positive and negative, or masculine
and feminine signs.

The first of these groupings, that of
the elements, comprises fire, earth,
air, and water signs. The second, that
of the qualities, divides the Zodiac

into cardinal, fixed, and mutable
signs. The final grouping is made up
of positive and negative, or masculine
and feminine signs. Each Zodiac sign
is associated with a combination of
components from these groupings, all
of which contribute different
characteristics to it.

Libran characteristics

Libra is a sign of the air element, and
there is a certain light airiness to the
Libran personality. People born under
this sign are usually able to
communicate with ease and are
pleasantly sociable.

The sign is of the cardinal quality,
which makes its subjects agreeable,
outgoing, warm, and charming. It is a
positive, masculine sign, and is
therefore likely to incline you toward
being extrovert. Venus is the sign's
ruling planet, and Libran colors
include pink, pale green, and
different shades of blue.

ARIES

PISCES

TAURUS

AQUARIUS

GEMINI

CAPRICORN

CANCER

SAGITTARIUS

LEO

SCORPIO

VIRGO

LIBRA

The Zodiac Wheel

The relationship between each Zodiac sign and the traditional astrological groupings is made clear within the Zodiac wheel. As you read through this book you will also discover references to polar, or opposite signs, and these, too, can be easily worked out by referring to the wheel.

FIRE

CARDINAL

EARTH

MASCULINE

MUTABLE

AIR

FEMININE

FIXED

WATER

9

LIBRA
MYTHS & LEGENDS

THE ZODIAC, WHICH MAY HAVE ORIGINATED IN BABYLON
AS LONG AS 2,500 YEARS AGO, IS A CIRCLE OF
CONSTELLATIONS THROUGH WHICH THE SUN MOVES
DURING THE COURSE OF A YEAR.

The constellation of Libra was celebrated in Babylon at least two thousand years before Christ, where it was connected to the myth of the last judgment and the weighing of souls. This is the earliest Libran association with scales. Later, the ancient Egyptians also weighed their harvest and assessed their taxes in autumn, at the time when the Babylonian judgment ceremony is believed to have taken place.

The Scorpion
In ancient times the claws of the Scorpion were recognized as occupying some of the area of the sky that is now set aside for Libra.

An ancient Babylonian name for Libra, ziba. anna, means the "horn" of a scorpion, which must actually be a reference to the creature's claws. Pictorially, these horns later developed into the scales of the balance that symbolizes Libra.

Weighing the soul
No myth is directly associated with Libra, but a single idea has been connected with the sign since at least ancient Egyptian times – that of a person's soul being weighed in the balance, after death.

The scene is shown in many illustrations in the Egyptian Book of the Dead. It features a man standing, often with his wife, beside the scales on which his heart is being weighed against a feather representing Truth. Anubis, the jackal-headed god of the dead, also known as Lord of the Mummy Wrappings, was believed to open up the roads to the afterlife for those who had died; the ancient Greeks associated him with their god, Hermes, the "Conductor of Souls." He often stands close to the scales, watching the judgment occurring. Thoth, the ibis-headed Egyptian moon-god, patron of science and literature, and of wisdom and

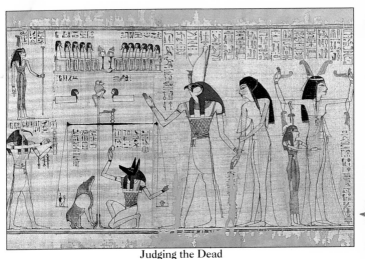

Judging the Dead

This scene from the Egyptian Book of the Dead, dating from 1100 B.C., shows Anubis, the jackal-headed god, and Thoth, the god of scribes, weighing a soul against Truth.

inventions, can also be seen nearby, meticulously noting down a faithful record of events.

The Bible

The conception of all the good in one's life being weighed against the sum of the evil, established by the ancient Egyptians, persisted into early Jewish culture. It is clearly reflected in the writings of what has come to be known as the Old Testament. In one passage from the Old Testament, the prophet Job asked that God "weigh him in the scales of justice," while Belshazzar was "weighed in the balance and found wanting."

Those people who are lucky enough to be born with the Sun in Libra are traditionally considered to have a particularly strong sense of justice and fairness.

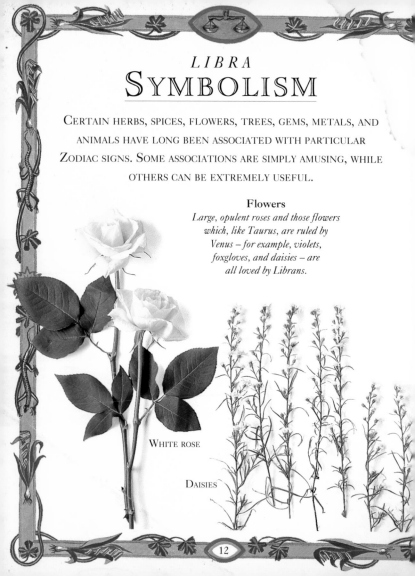

SYMBOLISM

CERTAIN HERBS, SPICES, FLOWERS, TREES, GEMS, METALS, AND
ANIMALS HAVE LONG BEEN ASSOCIATED WITH PARTICULAR
ZODIAC SIGNS. SOME ASSOCIATIONS ARE SIMPLY AMUSING, WHILE
OTHERS CAN BE EXTREMELY USEFUL.

Flowers

*Large, opulent roses and those flowers
which, like Taurus, are ruled by
Venus – for example, violets,
foxgloves, and daisies – are
all loved by Librans.*

WHITE ROSE

DAISIES

CYPRESS

Trees
The ash, the cypress, all vines, and those trees governed by Taurus, which shares the same ruling planet as Libra, are Libran trees.

SORREL

Herbs
Sorrel, which alleviates skin disorders, and figwort, which prevents blood clots, are all ruled by Libra.

Spices
No spices are particularly associated with Libra, but mace, and sometimes cloves and ginger, are generally popular among Librans.

CLOVES   GINGER

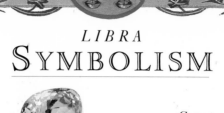

LIBRA
SYMBOLISM

YELLOW SAPPHIRE

Gems
The Libran gem is the sapphire. Some authorities also suggest chrysolite, a green gem.

COLORLESS
SAPPHIRE

PINK
SAPPHIRE

INDIAN TOY SNAKE

LIZARD BROOCH

LIZARD RING

14

Metal

Copper is a Libran metal, associated, like Taurus, with Venus. Bronze, an alloy of copper and tin, is also sometimes associated with the sign.

MIDDLE EASTERN
COPPER COFFEE POT

Animals

Lizards and small reptiles are traditionally associated with Libra. Snakes and many small domestic animals, such as mice and hamsters, are also sometimes linked with the sign.

SILVER SNAKE BROOCH

PROFILE

THERE IS AN ATTRACTIVE SOFTNESS TO THE LIBRAN IMAGE. THE
FEATURES MAY NOT BE VERY CLEAR-CUT.
PEOPLE OF THIS SIGN ARE USUALLY WELL DRESSED IN
THE CONTEXT OF THEIR PEER GROUP.

You might sometimes see Librans walking along, holding hands with their partners and looking affectionately at them, rather than at the road ahead. This invariably means that everything is right with their world. If, on the other hand, you see people of this sign slumping along the road, with their heads down and their hands deep in their pockets, you can assume that they lack love and affection. These signs of despondency usually mean that they are at a psychological low point.

The Libran face
Librans often appear gentle, and full of kindness and understanding.

The body
Provided you do what you can to increase your often rather slow metabolism, you will not lose your well-proportioned body and natural good looks, which contribute greatly to the enhancement of your charming personality. You may move gracefully, with a swinging gait, but are usually in no hurry. This explains your tendency to gain weight and your hesitancy in starting a diet.

The face
Libran men are inclined to have rather fine hair, and some of them are particularly prone to baldness. Your eyes are likely to show a capacity for kindness and understanding, and your nose is probably well proportioned in relation to the rest of your face. There is a tendency for the Libran chin to become less well defined with

The Libran stance

Librans often betray their uncertainty by shifting their weight from one foot to the other when in conversation.

increasing age and weight gain. You easily break into a gentle, sympathetic smile. Overall, the Libran expression often conveys a certain feyness. This usually has the effect of making the individual appear rather gentle.

Style

Librans generally have good taste in fashion. Pastel colors often suit both sexes. The women's image is rather pretty, with sexual allure, but not overt or vampish. An asymmetric line is sometimes favored, as are draped skirts. Rather light, delicate fabrics in pastel colors are often worn. These enhance the gentleness in the Libran image. Libran men, too, love to introduce a little romance into their clothes. They particularly like attractive, elaborately decorated shirts and unusual waistcoats. Hats are also very popular.

In general

The Libran stance can sometimes betray a degree of uncertainty. You may sometimes have a tendency to shift your weight from one foot to the other when you are speaking to someone. Similarly, when in conversation, you could sometimes hold your head first to one side, and then to the other. Bear in mind that people will not be slow in reading such body language.

In general, the gestures that you make tend to be quite slow, but they will always be meaningful and relatively uncomplicated.

PERSONALITY

LIBRANS ARE BOTH KIND AND WARMLY AFFECTIONATE. THEY HAVE
TIME FOR OTHER PEOPLE AND ARE NATURALLY GENEROUS.
THEIR NEED TO RELATE TO OTHERS CAN, HOWEVER, SOMETIMES
DRIVE THEM TO BUY FRIENDSHIP.

The Libran motivation might be summed up as a desire to keep life in balance and to relate in depth to another person.

Most Librans find loneliness almost intolerable and, until they are able to form a permanent relationship with someone, they are unlikely to be psychologically whole.

When you find yourself settled into a steady partnership, you will undergo a considerable blossoming of your Libran personality. It is, however, important for you to remember that a successful partnership is all about sharing. You must strive to keep the necessary balance and harmony that is typical of the Libran lifestyle.

At work

Librans are often lucky enough to possess the very pleasant ability to calm others and to help them unwind, giving the impression that time is no problem for them.

It is this tendency that has unfortunately given Librans in general a reputation for laziness. In fact, many of you are great achievers, who may well have reached top jobs in government, or perhaps the armed services. While Librans can sometimes be aggressive, they are also known to be peacemakers.

Your attitudes

Most Librans have the remarkably clever knack of seeing both sides of every problem. Because you understand your opponents' opinions, you may find it very difficult to draw final conclusions and come to constructive decisions. This is something that may cause you a variety of problems.

On the one hand, avoiding decisions can become so common for you that problems go away before they finally have to be faced. On the other hand, the same tendency can

Venus rules Libra

Venus, the Roman goddess of love, represents the ruling planet of both Libra and Taurus. The influence of Venus extends to art and fashion, and relates to the feminine side of a Libran's nature.

lead to immeasurable inconvenience to friends and family, who may never know quite where they stand, or what you actually plan to do and whether or not it will eventually be done.

The overall picture

While Librans are kind and do good things for others, it cannot be denied that they also enjoy receiving profuse thanks. Librans themselves are usually very forthcoming in this respect, so perhaps it is only natural that they expect the same reaction from other people. Some Zodiac types find it difficult to be even marginally gushing, but if a Libran merely receives a quiet "thank you" or, much worse, no thanks at all, resentfulness will soon set in.

LIBRA
ASPIRATIONS

YOU ARE A GREGARIOUS PERSON AND NEED COMPANY, SO
WORKING IN AN OPEN-PLAN OFFICE WILL HOLD NO
TERRORS. A POSITION OF AUTHORITY MAY NOT SUIT
YOU; YOU COULD FIND IT TOO LONELY.

Agent
*Librans have the ability to see both sides
of a situation, and therefore make
excellent agents in any area.*

APPOINTMENT DIARY

The legal profession
*Provided that they can
come to terms with their
indecisiveness, Librans
are people who are able
to ensure that justice
will be done.*

JUDGE'S GAVEL AND BLOCK

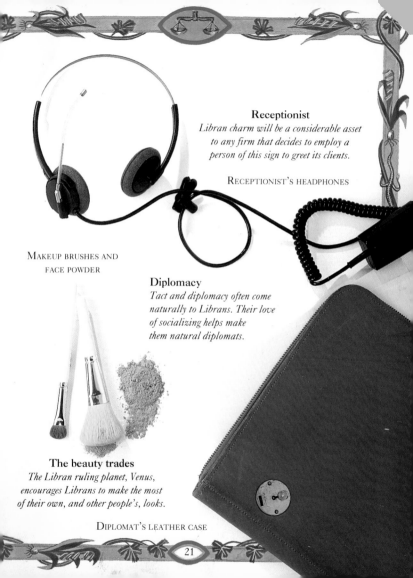

Receptionist
Libran charm will be a considerable asset to any firm that decides to employ a person of this sign to greet its clients.

RECEPTIONIST'S HEADPHONES

MAKEUP BRUSHES AND
FACE POWDER

Diplomacy
Tact and diplomacy often come naturally to Librans. Their love of socializing helps make them natural diplomats.

The beauty trades
The Libran ruling planet, Venus, encourages Librans to make the most of their own, and other people's, looks.

DIPLOMAT'S LEATHER CASE

LIBRA
HEALTH

IN ORDER FOR LIBRANS TO BE PHYSICALLY WELL, THEY NEED TO
LIVE WELL-BALANCED LIVES. UPSETTING ARGUMENTS AND
UNCOMFORTABLE LIVING CONDITIONS CANNOT BE TOLERATED
AND MUST BE AVOIDED AT ALL COSTS.

The delicate Libran system will be thrown into disarray by almost any kind of imbalance. This will often result in both mental and physical exhaustion, leading to headaches.

Your diet
As a Sun sign Libran you may need to supplement your diet with natrum phosphate (Nat. Phos.), which reduces acidity in the stomach. It prevents and helps to dissolve gallstones, and sometimes soothes an inflamed throat.

Many Librans have a rather slow metabolism. This, coupled with a preference for rich and often sweet food, can often lead to weight gain. Regular exercise is the solution to this problem.

Taking care
The Libran body area covers the kidneys. Should a headache strike unexpectedly, and if nothing has upset you, it may be that you are suffering from a slight kidney disorder. Perhaps, as with any unexpected health problem, you would be wise to receive a medical checkup. The lumbar region of the back can be somewhat vulnerable, and people in this Sun sign group would be wise to invest in a back-rest chair if they expect to spend a lot of time sitting at an office desk.

Red currants
*Berry fruits such as
red currants are
strongly associated
with Libra.*

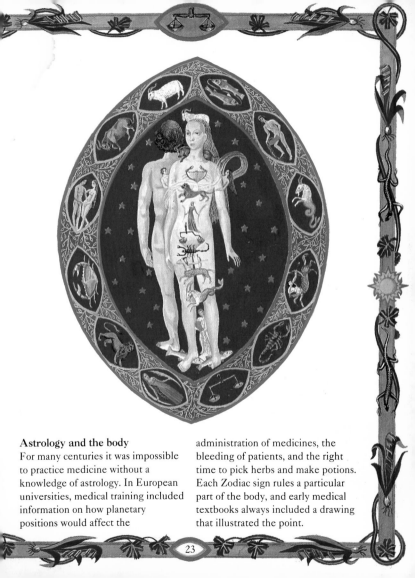

Astrology and the body

For many centuries it was impossible to practice medicine without a knowledge of astrology. In European universities, medical training included information on how planetary positions would affect the administration of medicines, the bleeding of patients, and the right time to pick herbs and make potions. Each Zodiac sign rules a particular part of the body, and early medical textbooks always included a drawing that illustrated the point.

LIBRA AT
LEISURE

Each of the Sun signs traditionally suggests spare-time activities, hobbies, and vacations. Although these are only suggestions, they often work out well, and reflect Libran interests.

Dressmaking

Librans who express their creativity through dressmaking may use their intuition to divine precisely the styles and colors that will be popular in the next season.

POSTAGE STAMPS

Travel

You will spend much time anticipating a month spent in Austria, Egypt, Burma, Japan, or even Tibet.

DRESSMAKING EQUIPMENT

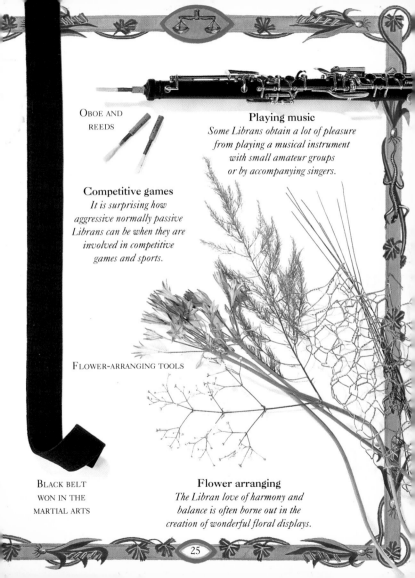

OBOE AND REEDS

Playing music
*Some Librans obtain a lot of pleasure
from playing a musical instrument
with small amateur groups
or by accompanying singers.*

Competitive games
*It is surprising how
aggressive normally passive
Librans can be when they are
involved in competitive
games and sports.*

FLOWER-ARRANGING TOOLS

**BLACK BELT
WON IN THE
MARTIAL ARTS**

Flower arranging
*The Libran love of harmony and
balance is often borne out in the
creation of wonderful floral displays.*

LIBRA IN LOVE

FOR LIBRANS, LIFE IS AT ITS MOST BEAUTIFUL WHEN THEY FALL
IN LOVE. THEY SHOULD, HOWEVER, ALWAYS REMEMBER TO
STOP AND CONSIDER WHETHER THEY ARE IN LOVE WITH THEIR
LOVER, OR WITH LOVE ITSELF.

The basic Libran motivation is to relate to another human being. Sharing, keeping life in balance, and living a harmonious life are all essential to you. More so than any other Zodiac type, a Libran who is alone will probably find life difficult to cope with and incomplete.

Although it might seem that a Libran's very indecisive nature could prevent commitment, this is in fact not usually the case. Librans are so eager to share and to relate that they often rush prematurely into a permanent relationship or marriage. Very often, of course, all is well, but if things go wrong, the resulting disruption to their lives can be far worse than it would be for people of any of the other Sun signs.

While in reality you are greatly in need of peace and harmony, many of you will try to pick fights with your partner just because it is so nice to kiss and make up afterward. Try not to take this too far, since such an attitude could be intensely wearing for your partners.

As a lover

It is the warmth and expression of really sincere affection that makes life with a Libran worthwhile.

Most of the time you will be in possession of the natural ability to create a delightful atmosphere that will doubtless enhance and color almost every aspect of the loving relationship which you enjoy with your partner.

Types of Libran lover

Some Librans have a great sense of drama. They enjoy making love in glamorous surroundings and have a tendency to look up to their partners. A second group is somewhat apprehensive about sex. These individuals are modest and romantic, but do not find it easy to relax into a relationship and can sometimes be very critical. The third group will agree with all of the comments made here. Their enjoyment of sex will develop gradually. Other Librans are deeply passionate, with a great need for sexual fulfillment. They can make very demanding partners, and must be careful not to act jealously. The final group is lively and enthusiastic about sex, and gets a great deal of sheer fun and pleasure from it. People in this group have a positive attitude, although they can be very flirtatious at times, and may even attempt dual relationships.

LIBRAN ROOMS ARE USUALLY HANDSOME, AND ENHANCED BY
FULL, HEAVY CURTAINS AND HANGINGS, PERHAPS IN
SHADES OF WARM PINK AND PALE BLUE. COMFORT IS A KEYNOTE,
AND IT IS BORNE OUT BY HUGE, WELCOMING CHAIRS.

Most Librans are very adaptable people who could probably set up a happy home in just about any kind of environment. The one place that is unlikely to appeal to them is a run-down district with very obvious signs of poverty and ugliness. Librans may also experience a great deal of unhappiness if they end up living miles from their nearest neighbors. No matter how happy they may be with their partners, loneliness could be a problem.

Elegant portraits
You may choose to display some elegantly framed antique photographs.

Furniture

Many Librans tend to favor traditional styles of furniture, and if some sweeping, well-balanced curves are integrated into the design, so much the better. Harsh, angular designs are not popular, since furniture like this often looks, and may even be, less than comfortable. There is no lack of elegance in the overall appearance of the home, or in individual pieces. For instance, fine legs will support occasional tables, as opposed to anything too heavy or solid. Few Librans like housework, but their sense of pride in their homes encourages them to get on with it.

Soft furnishings

Libra is a sign that positively wallows in soft furnishings. Cushions abound – they may even have been made by yourself. Curtains and drapes are of really lavish, rich velvet or lovely, printed floral satin with huge designs of roses. Austrian blinds are popular, and rugs will appear to be ankle deep. The colors are usually pastel, echoing those of Venus, the Libran ruling planet. A rich red or dark blue often makes an attractive contrast to these pale colors, and ensures that the overall effect is not too insipid.

Decorative objects

Librans are romantic, so objects that hint at love, for example heart-shaped pictures of your children, or of wedding groups, may be prominently displayed. The romantic theme often extends to your choice of paintings, and may be reflected in their soft colors or subject matter.

The emphasis that you will want to place upon stylish, cultured living will also be reflected in your paintings. A typical Libran choice might be a print of one of Gainsborough's portraits of beautiful women, an elegant painting of some flowers, or a set of prints depicting rare and exotic birds. If you actually collect prints or pictures, they will probably focus on fashion or on trades and professions from the past. A great many Librans like to collect

china or porcelain figures. These need not necessarily be antiques; they could just as easily be very attractive, but relatively inexpensive, graceful modern pieces. Even if you are not directly creative (and many Librans are) you are likely to have a great love of music and a highly developed appreciation of the arts. A musical instrument, most probably of the woodwind kind, may therefore provide the focal point of a decorative scheme in your home, even if you decide to simply leave it lying around until you can persuade someone else to play it.

Cushions and curtains
The Libran home will contain plenty of cushions and curtains made from sensuous velvets and satins.

THE
MOON
AND
YOU

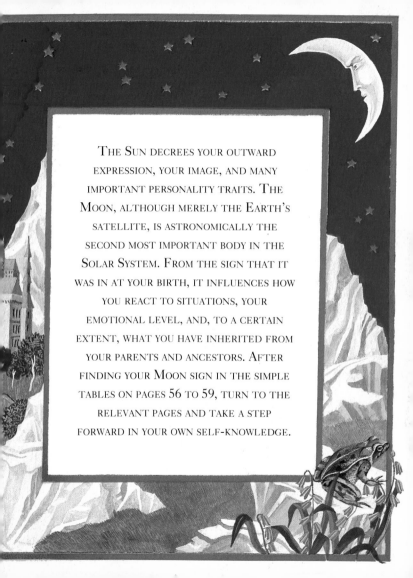

THE SUN DECREES YOUR OUTWARD
EXPRESSION, YOUR IMAGE, AND MANY
IMPORTANT PERSONALITY TRAITS. THE
MOON, ALTHOUGH MERELY THE EARTH'S
SATELLITE, IS ASTRONOMICALLY THE
SECOND MOST IMPORTANT BODY IN THE
SOLAR SYSTEM. FROM THE SIGN THAT IT
WAS IN AT YOUR BIRTH, IT INFLUENCES HOW
YOU REACT TO SITUATIONS, YOUR
EMOTIONAL LEVEL, AND, TO A CERTAIN
EXTENT, WHAT YOU HAVE INHERITED FROM
YOUR PARENTS AND ANCESTORS. AFTER
FINDING YOUR MOON SIGN IN THE SIMPLE
TABLES ON PAGES 56 TO 59, TURN TO THE
RELEVANT PAGES AND TAKE A STEP
FORWARD IN YOUR OWN SELF-KNOWLEDGE.

THE MOON IN
ARIES

LIBRA AND ARIES ARE POLAR ZODIAC SIGNS, SO YOU WERE BORN
UNDER A FULL MOON. RESTLESSNESS CAN SOMETIMES
BE A PROBLEM FOR YOU. WHEN YOU MEET WITH A CHALLENGE,
ALLOW YOUR ARIEN MOON TO STIR YOU TO ACTION.

Each of us, in one way or another, tends to express attributes of our polar sign (the opposite sign across the Zodiac circle from our Sun sign). For Librans, this is Aries, and since the Moon was in Aries when you were born, this "polarity" is emphasized in a very interesting way.

Self-expression
The typical indecisiveness of Libra is mitigated by your Arien Moon. Provided that you consciously control the tendency to act too quickly, your first reactions will often be correct. Therefore do not change your mind, however badly you are tempted.

Romance
Your Arien Moon bestows a wealth of positive emotion, which you no doubt express freely and passionately toward your partner. You are a romantic Libran, and your tendency to rush into a relationship is heightened by

your impulsive Moon.
You make a very rewarding partner, provided that you control selfishness, which is the worst Arien fault.

Your well-being
The fact that Libra and Aries are polar signs means that the relationship between the head (Aries) and the kidneys (Libra) is strongly emphasized. There are therefore two reasons why you may sometimes suffer from headaches. One may be psychologically based, while the other may be due to a mild kidney problem.

Aries is also prone to minor accidents, particularly cuts and burns. As a result you would be extremely wise to wear protective clothing whenever it is required.

Planning ahead
You have a wonderfully enterprising spirit, and provided that you do not allow your natural energy and

The Moon in Aries

enthusiasm to flag, you have what it takes to run a successful "sideline" business in addition to your main career. You will find such an interest extremely rewarding.

While you will be anxious to make your money work for you, make sure that you control impulsiveness when investing. You could, at times, get a little carried away. Remember, too, that it is not a good idea for you to put all your eggs in one basket just because of a burst of enthusiasm.

Parenthood

You respond positively and well to your children. You must, however, try very hard to be faithful to any decisions or opinions that you express. Otherwise they will be uncertain where they stand with you.

Your Arien Moon gives you the happy ability to tune in to your children's ideas and interests. If you express its lively qualities toward them, you will avoid problems with the generation gap.

THE MOON IN
TAURUS

LIBRA AND TAURUS ARE RULED BY THE PLANET VENUS, SO
THERE IS A NATURAL SYMPATHY BETWEEN THEM.
YOU LOVE COMFORT AND LUXURY, AND SHOULD USE YOUR
INTUITIVE BUSINESS SENSE TO PAY FOR THEM.

You have the ability to take life as it comes and to deal easily with worries, tension, and stress, giving others the impression that you are totally laid back. In many respects, you probably are. You certainly do not lack common sense, you pace yourself well, and you are less likely to get agitated than almost any Sun and Moon combination.

Self-expression

You may consciously have to nudge yourself when a swift answer or an immediate reaction is necessary. You much prefer to work deliberately through a problem, approaching it in a step-by-step fashion.

A slight problem is that while your Libran Sun encourages you to be fond of achieving peace at any price, your Taurean Moon inclines you to a predictable routine. When combined, the two influences may manage to edge you into a rut.

Romance

You are a very romantic, emotional Libran, and your Taurean Moon adds a warm sensuality and underlying passion to your personality that should be beautifully expressed toward your partners. You do, however, need a secure relationship; if you do not know where you stand with your partner you will not function well.

The worst Taurean fault is possessiveness. If this is combined with a Libran tendency to be slightly resentful, it could sometimes mar this vital area of your life. Let your Libran qualities give your partner the chance to breathe freely, and you will achieve a very rewarding life together.

Your well-being

The Taurean body area is the throat. With the onset of a cold, you could lose your voice and will certainly get a sore throat. A worse problem may be a slow metabolism and a love of rich

The Moon in Taurus

food. Try to regulate your eating habits and to discover some form of exercise that you enjoy.

Planning ahead

You should have excellent intuition where money is concerned, and will probably be able to watch the figures in your bank book grow steadily and satisfactorily. However, the luxuries that you enjoy so much will be expensive. Go all out for a regular pay check, and invest when you can. Use your great intuition in these matters.

Parenthood

Do not let Libran indecision and Taurean possessiveness encroach on your relationship with your children. You will work hard for them, but you could be rather conservative in your attitude to their opinions and concerns. Make a conscious effort to understand their problems and you will avoid the generation gap. You will certainly give your children a good, secure background and will be kind and thoughtful. You must, however, remember to have fun, too.

THE MOON IN
GEMINI

BOTH LIBRA AND GEMINI ARE AIR SIGNS, SO IN ADDITION
TO BEING SYMPATHETIC AND CHARMING, YOU ARE A
GOOD COMMUNICATOR. BE CAREFUL, HOWEVER, THAT
YOU DO NOT SUPPRESS YOUR DEEPER EMOTIONS.

The air element forms a large part of your personality. You have a lightness about you; a certain breezy but logical approach to problems. When challenged, you will always have flip, off-the-cuff verbal responses on hand.

Self-expression

You find conversation and social intercourse even more rewarding and entertaining than most Sun sign Librans and may well make a real hobby of entertaining your friends.

To prevent Geminian restlessness, try to develop a compelling and rewarding interest. Take care that you do not simply glide over the surface of important problems because you do not wish to get too involved.

Romance

Your love of romance will be very well expressed verbally, and to a certain extent you need a high level of friendship within an emotional relationship. While you are as romantic as any Libran, you may not be able to allow your deepest feelings to flow as freely as would be ideal.

Aim for partners who will be intellectually challenging to live with, so that your extremely lively mind will be kept active.

Your well-being

The Geminian body area covers the arms and hands, and yours may be somewhat vulnerable to accidents. The Geminian organ is the lungs, and anyone with this sign emphasized should try not to smoke.

Usually, Moon sign Geminians tend to be restless, but you should suffer less than most in this respect because of your Libran Sun. You may well enjoy exercise more than most Sun sign Librans, and this could take the form of tennis, badminton, or some other fast game. Because you

The Moon in Gemini

probably have a higher metabolic rate than many Librans, and may not have the typical taste for sweet food, you are less likely to incur excessive weight gain.

Planning ahead

As far as coping with money is concerned, you may not be terribly practical. You love luxury and are generous, but money could very easily burn a hole in your pocket, and you may be attracted to get-rich-quick schemes. Take professional financial advice in this area, and make sure that you never lay out more money than you can afford to lose.

Parenthood

You have a modern outlook, of which your children will no doubt thoroughly approve. Keeping up with their opinions and concerns will therefore be no problem for you. Provided you are firm and decisive, so that your children know where they stand, you will have no problems with the generation gap.

THE MOON IN
CANCER

YOU ARE VERY GOOD AT LISTENING TO PEOPLE, BUT COULD
THROW YOUR SYSTEM OUT OF BALANCE BY TAKING ON
OTHERS' BURDENS. WATCH OUT FOR STRESS, AND BE AWARE
THAT YOU MAY BENEFIT FROM PHYSICAL EXERCISE.

Both Libra and Cancer are of the cardinal quality, which means that you have the ability to sympathize and empathize with others, and will give of yourself to help and comfort them. Your instinct is to protect and care for your family and friends, and you do more than your fair share to help people feel good. Do not burn yourself out, emotionally or intellectually.

Self-expression

In spite of having a great deal of inner strength, you can be very easily hurt. Although you can be extremely kind, you can sometimes express yourself rather sharply, and say things that insult others. Be aware of this. It would be a pity to let such a negative trait mar your finer qualities.

You are probably very prone to worry – far more, in fact, than most Librans. You do, however, have very powerful instincts, and can use them

to counter this problem. If you feel that you should take a certain line of action, go ahead and do so.

Romance

You are a wonderfully romantic and sensual lover, and should enjoy a rich and fulfilling sex life. Try, however, not to be overprotective of your partners. You may well create a rather claustrophobic atmosphere, which some people will find hard to cope with. Whether you are a man or a woman, you may occasionally tend to "mother" your partners.

Your well-being

The Cancerian body area covers the chest and breasts. Although there is no connection between this sign and the disease of the same name, regular checkups are always a good idea.

The Cancerian tendency to worry may have a negative effect on your health. Your food could tend to

The Moon in Cancer

disagree with you when you are worried. If you can keep this negative emotion under control, your digestion will be far less likely to suffer.

Planning ahead

Like all people of your Sun sign, you like luxury and creature comforts, but you are less extravagant than many Librans and have a natural instinct to be careful with money. You also have a shrewd business sense that will work well for you whether you have your own business or have merely collected a little spare money that you want to invest.

Parenthood

You make a wonderfully caring parent and will enjoy bringing up your children, although their natural exuberance and energy may tend to deflate you at times.

If you make a conscious effort to be decisive, and do your best to avoid sentimentality or dwelling on the past, you will have few problems with the generation gap. You must try not to get too upset when your children leave home to build their own lives. Rather than moping, take the opportunity to become involved in some new interests.

THE MOON IN
LEO

YOU LIKE EVERYTHING THAT IS EXPENSIVE. YOU ARE ALSO WARM,
SYMPATHETIC, BIG-HEARTED, AND GENEROUS, BUT IF YOU
ACT ON YOUR IMAGINATIVE IDEAS WITHOUT SERIOUSLY COUNTING
THE COST, YOU COULD GET INTO TROUBLE.

The combination of Libra and Leo is a good one. It makes your outlook very positive and optimistic. Much more so than many of your Sun sign compatriots, you will "think big" and be magnanimous.

Self-expression

Anyone with an emphasis on Leo has creative potential and, while this is not always expressed through the fine arts, it is nevertheless present. It is important to your sense of inner fulfillment that some form of creativity play a part in your life.

You are an excellent organizer and can readily take over in a crisis. You should enjoy work that gives you the chance to show off a little and, if Libran diplomacy is combined with Leo warmth, you can probably cope well with people and their problems.

Your Leo Moon gives you a sense of drama, but be careful not to overstep the mark. Do not make a dramatic scene over something trivial that displeases or upsets you. Calm authority is more effective.

Romance

You have a wealth of positive emotion to express toward your partners, and you want to feel proud of them.

Beware of the tendency to fall in love with love. You can be very easily hurt and, when you are, you will retire to a private lair to lick your wounds.

Your well-being

The Leo body area covers the spine and back. You must therefore make sure that you always sit correctly. A support chair is advisable for desk workers, and back-strengthening exercises are good for anyone with this emphasis.

The Leo organ is the heart, and it must be kept well toned. Therefore take regular exercise; dancing is excellent if you hate the thought of

The Moon in Leo

sports or health clubs.

Both Libra and Leo like to live the good life. This all too often means lots of rich food and, in turn, a weight problem. Try to ration the sauces and elaborate desserts.

Planning ahead

You are more than likely to be both very generous and very extravagant. It should therefore come as no surprise for you to realize that you will consequently need to earn a lot of money in order to support such habits. Quality is also important to you, so at least the things that you

buy will last a long time. You could tend to over invest at times, and you may benefit from professional advice.

Parenthood

You will probably be an enthusiastic and very encouraging parent, and will be constantly delighted with your children's efforts. Spurred on by your encouragement, they will want to do even more to please you.

Be careful that you do not change your mind too often, once you have told your children something. It is extremely important for them to know where they stand with you.

THE MOON IN
VIRGO

YOUR MOON SIGN CAN CAUSE YOU TO BE MORE SPONTANEOUSLY
AND HARSHLY CRITICAL OF OTHERS THAN YOU MAY
REALIZE. WHILE IT MAKES YOU PRACTICAL, IT CAN ALSO MAR
SOME FINE LIBRAN QUALITIES.

You may express your Libran loving-kindness very well, but you will, under some circumstances, also respond in a very critical manner. Perhaps you should try to be a little more tactful and diplomatic.

Self-expression

Your Virgoan Moon certainly gives you a lot more energy than many Sun sign Librans, and you are unlikely to waste much time.

Your initial reaction to a difficult situation may be to worry about it. Very soon, however, your attitude will take a turn toward being much more relaxed and philosophical.

You can use your Virgoan Moon to help you overcome Libran indecision. You could, for instance, analyze problems by making comprehensive lists of their positive and negative aspects, and then considering them in as detached, logical, and unemotional fashion as you are able.

Romance

Although you will certainly work very hard for your partners, and give them excellent backup, you may not find it easy to unlock your emotions and really relax. Although you are as romantic as anyone of your Sun sign, it may not be easy for you to enjoy love and sex wholeheartedly. Be very careful not to overcriticize your partner or to nag.

Your well-being

The Virgoan body area is the stomach, and it is possible that this reacts very quickly to the least worry or concern. You probably need a high-fiber diet.

Many people with this combination of signs have a fast metabolism; in these cases the tendency to put on weight is minimized. If you do move rather slowly, be careful not to eat too much heavy food. Conversely, if you are working very hard, try to make sure that you have a well-balanced

The Moon in Virgo

diet, and do not eat too much junk food. Aim for a fairly light diet that contains salads and fresh fruit.

Like many people with a Virgoan emphasis, you may be a vegetarian. If this is the case, make certain that your vitamin intake is adequate.

Planning ahead

You love your Libran luxuries, but will not waste money and will generally have enough for your needs. Making investments could, however, be rather boring for you, so keep them simple and take professional advice if you wish to invest a large sum of cash.

Parenthood

As a parent you are kind and generous, but you must watch a tendency to sometimes speak to your children rather harshly.

You are a good communicator and find it easy to get your ideas across. Listen to your children, and you will avoid generation gap problems.

THE MOON IN
LIBRA

BOTH THE SUN AND THE MOON WERE IN LIBRA AT THE TIME OF
YOUR BIRTH, AND YOU WERE THEREFORE BORN UNDER A NEW
MOON. YOU HAVE MANY LIBRAN CHARACTERISTICS AND RESPOND
TO MOST SITUATIONS IN A BALANCED AND HARMONIOUS WAY.

Should you read a list of the characteristics of your Libran Sun sign, you will probably realize that a great many of them apply to you. On average, out of a list of around 20 personality traits attributed to a sign, most people accept 11 or 12. For you the average will be much higher, since both the Sun and the Moon were in Libra when you were born.

Self-expression
You need to lead a well-balanced, harmonious life, and find quarrels very upsetting.

You always respond to situations by first considering the other people involved, and never give priority to your own considerations or opinions. This can make you very indecisive and, at times, you may well avoid a commitment simply by mulling over a situation for so long that a decision becomes unnecessary. You are very diplomatic, and respond kindly and

affectionately to people around you. They will love you for your natural charm and delightful personality.

Romance
Your need to relate to another person is instinctive and runs very deep. You will be psychologically whole only when settled in a permanent relationship or marriage. It is in this area that Libran indecision can totally desert you, and you can very easily rush prematurely into a relationship just because you feel that you need one badly. A degree of objectivity could well save a lot of heartache.

Your well-being
Everything that has been said about Libran health on pages 22 – 23 will probably apply to you. You must keep your whole system balanced with steady exercise, and should refrain from overindulgence in food or drink. Your thoughts and emotions must

The Moon in Libra

remain at one, and you should try to avoid arguments. Learn to have your say calmly and effectively.

Planning ahead
Your creature comforts are important to you, and you will spend a lot of money on them.

You are inclined to be naturally generous and may not be terribly practical when it comes to handling money. You will probably do well to consult a professional adviser if you have money to invest.

Parenthood
You will enjoy a warm, affectionate rapport with your children and will be very kind to them. Force yourself to be decisive, and do not spoil your children for the sake of peace and quiet. They need a constructive framework and fair discipline. If you make sure that your children know where they stand with you, you will be an excellent parent.

As long as you remain interested in your children's ideas and concerns, you will bridge the generation gap.

THE MOON IN
SCORPIO

YOU RESPOND TO MOST SITUATIONS WITH GREATER EMOTIONAL
FERVOR AND INTENSITY THAN MANY LIBRANS, AND YOU
HAVE IT IN YOU TO TAKE STRONG, DECISIVE ACTION. DO NOT
SUPPRESS THIS QUALITY; LISTEN TO YOUR INTUITION.

Your Scorpio Moon gives you more determination and a stronger sense of purpose than many Sun sign Librans. You have a powerfully inquiring mind and, when challenged, strong forces immediately come into play in order to help you combat opposition.

Self-expression
Your opponents will get as good, or better, as they give, but it is important that you do not later backtrack and overapologize to them. This can upset the status quo, and lead to disruption and even quarrels, which your Libran Sun sign positively hates.

You must also aim to be emotionally involved in your work. An "ordinary" job, or drifting from one job to the next in an aimless fashion, will not do at all. Go all out for what you want to do, and do not let Libran hesitancy or indecision bog you down. You have powerful reserves of

emotional energy and the ability to express them very positively through your chosen career or some other compelling interest.

Romance
You will be a demanding partner, but one who contributes greatly to a relationship. Like all Librans, you are a romantic, but you are far more passionate and highly sexed than many people of your Sun sign.

The worst Scorpio fault is jealousy. Be very careful, as you could become a victim of this very negative emotional expression.

Your well-being
The Scorpio body area is the genitals, and both men and women should pay attention to the health of that area.

You may have a tendency to bottle up your problems. When worried, make sure that you unburden yourself to a sympathetic friend.

The Moon in Scorpio

Planning ahead

Your Scorpio Moon is beneficial to you when it comes to dealing with money. It is likely to make you a shrewd and clever investor.

Anyone with a strong Scorpio influence will, however, want to both get a lot out of life and put a lot into it. This usually means resorting to heavy spending. Therefore look for savings schemes that make your money grow and work for you. You are clever enough not to make many mistakes, even if you do not take professional advice, but you may well need to curb extravagance.

Parenthood

You will have strong views about bringing up your children, but your more placid, Libran qualities could persuade you to spoil them.

Make sure that you keep up with your children's opinions and concerns. Otherwise you may encounter problems with the generation gap.

THE MOON IN
SAGITTARIUS

YOU ARE EASYGOING AND HAVE MUCH INTELLECTUAL POTENTIAL.
TO MAKE IT WORK FOR YOU, YOU SHOULD KEEP MOVING,
BOTH PHYSICALLY AND MENTALLY. DO NOT IMMEDIATELY BRUSH
ASIDE OTHER PEOPLE'S SUGGESTIONS.

The two elements of your Sun and Moon signs, air and fire, respectively, will work to your benefit. You will always have a very positive and philosophical outlook on life, and will not, on the whole, be plagued by worry or tension.

Self-expression

You like to be challenged and, upon encountering difficult situations or problems, you are always optimistic about their outcome. Your Moon sign gives you a very natural, instinctive optimism that harmonizes extremely well with your Libran qualities, but be careful not to be too laid back.

You may have a natural flair for study and could actually need this particular kind of challenge.

Romance

You have very lively and fiery emotions, and are capable of a marvelously exuberant enjoyment of love and sex. You may not always take this sphere of your life very seriously and, unlike many people of your Sun sign, you will have a strong need for independence within a relationship. As a result, you will be far less likely to rush into a commitment, in spite of all your buoyant enthusiasm. You also have something of a roving eye, and should remember that this is not necessarily a very good thing, especially in relation to love.

Your well-being

The Sagittarian body areas are the hips and thighs, and women with this sign emphasized may put on weight easily in these areas. You need more exercise than most Librans, and will perhaps enjoy the challenge of keeping fit. Maintain a steady exercise routine.

The Sagittarian organ is the liver, and anyone with a Libra and Sagittarius combination will enjoy

The Moon in Sagittarius

their food. Therefore be careful, since you are no doubt very prone to overeating and hangovers.

Planning ahead
Your Sagittarian Moon gives you a powerful gambling instinct, so beware of casinos and racetracks.

You may also be very attracted to investments that make promises of high returns on your capital. Control your enthusiasm, or you could well lose out. The same applies when a get-rich-quick scheme is put to you. Develop skepticism and always seek professional advice.

You are very generous, but should remember that it is better to give someone a few dollars than to lend them a lot, since the chances are that you will not see your money again.

Parenthood
Your Sagittarian Moon will make it easy for you to encourage your children in all their interests and studies. You will enjoy their company, and there will be an element of fun in your relationship. You will not find it difficult to keep up with your children's views and opinions, and will thus avoid the generation gap.

THE MOON IN
CAPRICORN

YOU HAVE AN INNER DESIRE TO REACH THE TOP, BOTH SOCIALLY
AND IN YOUR CAREER. TRY NOT TO SHOW OFF. ALLOW YOUR
PRACTICAL, EARTHY MOON SIGN INSTINCTS TO STEADY YOU AND
KEEP YOUR PERSONALITY IN BALANCE.

Both Libra and Capricorn are of the cardinal quality and, as a result, you may use your energies to encourage others. You will respond practically to their problems, and will cope extremely well in emergencies.

Self-expression
You may take life more seriously than many Librans. Some of the time you will feel positive and optimistic; at other times you may succumb to negative feelings.

You are probably very ambitious and a hard worker, even if you give the impression of being relaxed. You will pack a lot into the working day and, with persistence of effort, will achieve a great deal.

Romance
Libra is a warm, romantic sign, while Capricorn is rather unemotional and cool. You cope well with solitude; better, in fact, than most Librans.

When you share your life with a partner, you may need to spend some time alone.

Once committed to a partner you will be faithful, but may be a little grudging in expressing your affections. Allow your Libran Sun to counter this tendency, and relax.

Your well-being
The Capricornian body area covers the knees and shins, which are therefore vulnerable.

The skin and teeth are also ruled by Capricorn. Your skin may be more sensitive to the sun than most people's, so wear a protective cream in summer. Do not neglect your regular dental checkups, either.

You may be less attracted to sweet food than many Librans and will therefore be less prone to weight gain. A tendency to incur stiffness of the joints means that you will probably benefit from exercise.

The Moon in Capricorn

Planning ahead

You are likely to be more careful when it comes to handling money than many Librans, and will no doubt tend to opt for quality in what you buy. You may spend a lot of money on impressing other people, perhaps by entertaining them lavishly.

Social climbing may be something of a hobby with you. This is fine, but it could cost you dearly and will not always have the desired effect. You will invest wisely and probably have a sensible attitude to finance in general.

Concentrate on maintaining steady growth from sound, even unadventurous, investments.

Parenthood

Although you are in many ways warm and affectionate, there will be periods when you may not have time for your children. You could find it difficult to keep up with their ideas, perhaps because you are rather conventional in outlook. Try to counter this tendency, or it could well cause generation gap problems.

THE MOON IN
AQUARIUS

BOTH LIBRA AND AQUARIUS ARE AIR SIGNS. TOGETHER THEY
GIVE YOU ORIGINALITY AND CHARM. YOU MAY, HOWEVER,
NEED TO DEVELOP A MORE PRACTICAL AND SERIOUS APPROACH
TO SOME SPHERES OF LIFE.

There is a delightful friendly and lighthearted area of your personality that immediately rises to the surface whenever you come into contact with other people.

Self-expression
Your manner is open and positive, and you are very gregarious. More than most Librans, you possess an independent streak which ensures that you do things in your own way. You have a great deal of individuality, which may be expressed creatively.

Surprisingly, you could sometimes react to situations rather stubbornly and can be very unpredictable. Try to control these tendencies, for while they can be amusing, they can also cause disruption and annoyance.

Romance
Libra and Aquarius are the two signs with the greatest inclination for real romance. Your Aquarian Moon will contribute glamour, but will also cool the emotions. You are attractive to the opposite sex, but may tend to keep people at a distance. In doing so, you will be expressing Aquarian independence, but also acting against your Libran need to relate. You need a partner who understands these areas of your personality, and who will encourage you to express your emotions freely.

Your well-being
The Aquarian body area is the ankles. You may find yourself turning your ankle all too often, which will cause you considerable discomfort.

Aquarius also rules the circulation, and you may well feel the cold very badly. Conversely, you may suffer when it is hot. Exercise is necessary to keep your circulation in good order. You could get bored with many forms of it, but should enjoy tennis, dance, or winter sports. You could

The Moon in Aquarius

participate in a variety of physical activities, changing them according to the different seasons.

Planning ahead
You have an eye for beautiful things and may end up spending a lot of money on them. Do, however, choose carefully. Many things increase in value and therefore make good investments; others lose their value. Because you are attracted to the unusual and glamorous, you could invest your funds unwisely. Always obtain financial advice when you have money to put aside, and try to save regularly.

Parenthood
You should not suffer from the generation gap as your children grow up, because you are always attracted to the new. Do, however, make a solid effort to curb unpredictability, since it is vital that your children know where they stand in relation to you.

THE MOON IN
PISCES

YOUR RESPONSE TO DIFFICULT SITUATIONS MAY BE TO TAKE THE
PATH OF LEAST RESISTANCE. DOING SO COULD, HOWEVER,
HURT OTHERS FAR MORE THAN YOU REALIZE, THEREBY UPSETTING
YOUR PRIZED HARMONIOUS LIFESTYLE.

The combination of your Sun and Moon signs makes you an extremely kind, gentle, and magnanimous person.

Self-expression

Without hesitating, you will offer help as soon as you see that it is needed and will often inconvenience yourself in order to do so. You must try to distance yourself from emotional and psychological involvement in such cases, while at the same time retaining your sympathetic and understanding rapport.

You may need to develop a sense of purpose and greater determination if you have an inclination to drift. The real reason for this tendency may be a certain lack of self-confidence.

Romance

You have a high emotional level that you will be able to express in your relationships. You will make a wonderfully caring partner, but may become a far too willing slave. Remember that partnership is about sharing. Keep your balance, and try to develop a relationship with someone who will be strong enough to lean on, but who will also recognize your talents, encourage your efforts, and help you to organize your life.

Your well-being

The Piscean body area is the feet. Your feet are therefore vulnerable to blisters, corns, and other ailments.

You are also sensitive to prevailing atmospheres. Bad ones could cause stomach upsets, as will worry, to which you may be more susceptible than many Sun sign Librans.

Planning ahead

You really are a soft touch where money is concerned. You need someone to control your finances with a rod of iron; otherwise you may end

The Moon in Pisces

up being too generous. There are, however, certain things that you can do for yourself. You can take part in a savings plan in which the contributions are taken out of your paycheck. You would be wise never to lend money and should try not to give too much of it away.

Your artistic and creative potential could well prove to be exceptionally lucrative. You should, however, concentrate on producing the raw product, and leave the difficult and specialized task of balancing the books to someone who is much more proficient at it than you.

Parenthood

As a parent, you may tend to spoil your children badly when they are young. This could be partly to buy yourself peace and quiet. Be decisive, and do not keep changing your mind when your children need direction from you. It is important for them to know where they stand with you.

You will not find it too difficult to enjoy your children's interests, and as a result you should not incur problems with the generation gap. However, never let your children twist you around their little fingers, as they will certainly try to do.

MOON CHARTS

THE FOLLOWING TABLES WILL ENABLE YOU TO DISCOVER YOUR
MOON SIGN. THEN, BY REFERRING TO THE PRECEDING
PAGES, YOU WILL BE ABLE TO INVESTIGATE ITS QUALITIES, AND
SEE HOW THEY WORK WITH YOUR SUN SIGN.

By referring to the charts on pages 57, 58 and 59 locate the Zodiacal glyph for the month of the year in which you were born. Using the Moon table on this page, find the number opposite the day you were born that month. Then, starting from the glyph you found first, count off that number using the list of Zodiacal glyphs (below, right). You may have to count to Pisces and continue with Aries. For example, if you were born on May 21, 1991, first you need to find the Moon sign on the chart on page 59. Look down the chart to May; the glyph is Sagittarius (♐). Then consult the Moon table for the 21st. It tells you to add nine glyphs. Starting from Sagittarius, count down nine, and you find your Moon sign is Virgo (♍).

MOON TABLE

DAYS OF THE MONTH AND NUMBER OF
SIGNS THAT SHOULD BE ADDED

DAY	ADD	DAY	ADD	DAY	ADD	DAY	ADD
1	0	9	4	17	7	25	11
2	1	10	4	18	8	26	11
3	1	11	5	19	8	27	12
4	1	12	5	20	9	28	12
5	2	13	5	21	9	29	1
6	2	14	6	22	10	30	1
7	3	15	6	23	10	31	2
8	3	16	7	24	10		

ZODIACAL GLYPHS

♈	Aries
♉	Taurus
♊	Gemini
♋	Cancer
♌	Leo
♍	Virgo
♎	Libra
♏	Scorpio
♐	Sagittarius
♑	Capricorn
♒	Aquarius
♓	Pisces

	1923	1924	1925	1926	1927	1928	1929	1930	1931	1932	1933	1934	1935
JAN	♊	♏	♈	♌	♐	♈	♍	♑	♉	♎	♓	♋	♏
FEB	♌	♐	♉	♍	♑	♊	♏	♓	♋	♐	♈	♌	♑
MAR	♌	♑	♉	♍	♒	♋	♏	♓	♋	♐	♉	♍	♑
APR	♎	♓	♋	♏	♈	♍	♑	♉	♍	♒	♊	♎	♓
MAY	♏	♈	♌	♐	♉	♎	♒	♊	♎	♓	♋	♐	♈
JUN	♑	♉	♍	♒	♋	♏	♓	♌	♐	♉	♍	♑	♊
JUL	♒	♋	♏	♓	♌	♐	♈	♍	♑	♊	♎	♓	♋
AUG	♈	♌	♐	♉	♍	♒	♊	♏	♓	♋	♐	♈	♌
SEP	♉	♎	♒	♋	♏	♓	♌	♐	♈	♍	♑	♊	♎
OCT	♊	♏	♓	♌	♐	♉	♍	♑	♉	♎	♓	♋	♏
NOV	♌	♑	♉	♍	♑	♊	♏	♓	♋	♐	♈	♌	♑
DEC	♍	♒	♊	♎	♓	♌	♐	♈	♌	♑	♉	♍	♒

	1936	1937	1938	1939	1940	1941	1942	1943	1944	1945	1946	1947	1948
JAN	♈	♌	♑	♉	♍	♒	♊	♎	♓	♌	♐	♈	♍
FEB	♉	♎	♒	♊	♏	♈	♌	♐	♉	♍	♑	♊	♎
MAR	♊	♎	♒	♋	♐	♈	♌	♐	♉	♎	♒	♊	♏
APR	♌	♐	♈	♌	♑	♉	♎	♒	♋	♏	♓	♌	♑
MAY	♍	♑	♉	♎	♒	♊	♏	♓	♌	♐	♉	♍	♒
JUN	♎	♒	♋	♏	♈	♌	♑	♉	♎	♒	♊	♏	♓
JUL	♏	♈	♌	♑	♉	♍	♒	♊	♏	♓	♌	♐	♈
AUG	♑	♉	♎	♒	♋	♏	♈	♌	♐	♉	♍	♑	♊
SEP	♓	♋	♏	♈	♌	♑	♉	♍	♒	♋	♏	♓	♌
OCT	♈	♌	♑	♉	♎	♒	♊	♎	♓	♌	♐	♈	♍
NOV	♊	♎	♒	♊	♏	♈	♌	♐	♉	♍	♑	♊	♏
DEC	♋	♏	♓	♌	♑	♉	♍	♑	♊	♎	♒	♋	♐

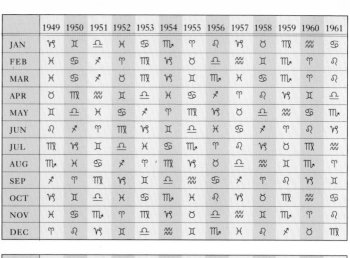

	1949	1950	1951	1952	1953	1954	1955	1956	1957	1958	1959	1960	1961
JAN	♑	♊	♎	♓	♋	♏	♈	♌	♑	♉	♍	♒	♋
FEB	♓	♋	♐	♈	♍	♑	♉	♎	♒	♊	♏	♈	♌
MAR	♓	♋	♐	♉	♍	♑	♊	♏	♓	♋	♏	♈	♌
APR	♉	♍	♒	♊	♎	♓	♋	♐	♈	♌	♑	♊	♎
MAY	♊	♎	♓	♋	♐	♈	♍	♑	♉	♎	♒	♋	♏
JUN	♌	♐	♈	♍	♑	♊	♎	♓	♋	♐	♈	♌	♑
JUL	♍	♑	♊	♎	♓	♋	♏	♈	♌	♑	♉	♍	♒
AUG	♏	♓	♋	♐	♈	♍	♑	♉	♎	♒	♊	♏	♈
SEP	♐	♈	♍	♑	♊	♎	♒	♋	♐	♈	♌	♑	♊
OCT	♑	♊	♎	♓	♋	♏	♓	♌	♑	♉	♍	♒	♋
NOV	♓	♋	♏	♈	♍	♑	♉	♎	♒	♊	♏	♈	♌
DEC	♈	♌	♑	♊	♎	♒	♊	♏	♓	♌	♐	♉	♍

	1962	1963	1964	1965	1966	1967	1968	1969	1970	1971	1972	1973	1974
JAN	♏	♓	♌	♐	♈	♍	♑	♊	♎	♒	♋	♐	♈
FEB	♐	♉	♍	♒	♊	♏	♓	♋	♏	♈	♍	♑	♉
MAR	♐	♉	♎	♒	♊	♏	♈	♌	♐	♉	♍	♑	♊
APR	♒	♋	♏	♈	♌	♑	♉	♍	♒	♊	♏	♓	♋
MAY	♓	♌	♐	♉	♍	♒	♊	♎	♓	♋	♐	♈	♍
JUN	♉	♎	♒	♊	♏	♓	♌	♐	♉	♍	♑	♊	♎
JUL	♊	♏	♓	♌	♐	♈	♍	♑	♊	♎	♓	♋	♐
AUG	♌	♐	♉	♎	♒	♊	♏	♓	♋	♏	♈	♍	♑
SEP	♍	♒	♋	♏	♓	♋	♐	♉	♍	♑	♊	♎	♓
OCT	♏	♓	♌	♐	♈	♍	♒	♊	♎	♒	♋	♐	♈
NOV	♐	♉	♎	♒	♊	♎	♓	♋	♐	♈	♍	♑	♉
DEC	♑	♊	♏	♓	♋	♐	♈	♌	♑	♉	♎	♒	♊

	1975	1976	1977	1978	1979	1980	1981	1982	1983	1984	1985	1986	1987
JAN	♌	♑	♉	♍	♒	♊	♏	♓	♌	♐	♉	♍	♑
FEB	♎	♒	♋	♏	♈	♌	♐	♉	♍	♒	♊	♎	♓
MAR	♎	♓	♋	♏	♈	♍	♑	♉	♎	♒	♊	♏	♓
APR	♐	♈	♍	♑	♊	♎	♒	♋	♏	♈	♌	♑	♉
MAY	♑	♉	♎	♒	♋	♏	♓	♌	♐	♉	♍	♒	♊
JUN	♓	♋	♐	♈	♌	♑	♉	♎	♒	♊	♏	♓	♌
JUL	♈	♌	♑	♉	♍	♒	♋	♏	♓	♌	♐	♉	♍
AUG	♉	♎	♓	♋	♏	♈	♌	♐	♈	♎	♒	♊	♎
SEP	♋	♐	♈	♌	♐	♊	♎	♒	♊	♏	♓	♌	♐
OCT	♌	♑	♉	♍	♒	♋	♏	♓	♋	♐	♉	♍	♑
NOV	♎	♓	♋	♏	♓	♌	♐	♉	♍	♒	♊	♎	♓
DEC	♏	♈	♌	♐	♉	♍	♑	♊	♎	♓	♋	♐	♈

	1988	1989	1990	1991	1992	1993	1994	1995	1996	1997	1998	1999	2000
JAN	♊	♎	♒	♋	♏	♈	♌	♑	♉	♎	♒	♊	♏
FEB	♋	♐	♈	♍	♑	♉	♎	♒	♋	♏	♈	♌	♐
MAR	♌	♐	♉	♍	♒	♊	♎	♓	♋	♏	♈	♌	♑
APR	♍	♒	♊	♏	♓	♋	♐	♈	♍	♑	♊	♎	♓
MAY	♏	♓	♌	♐	♈	♍	♑	♉	♎	♒	♋	♏	♈
JUN	♐	♉	♍	♑	♊	♎	♓	♋	♐	♈	♌	♑	♉
JUL	♑	♊	♎	♒	♋	♐	♈	♌	♑	♉	♎	♒	♋
AUG	♓	♌	♐	♈	♍	♑	♉	♎	♓	♋	♏	♓	♌
SEP	♉	♍	♑	♊	♏	♓	♋	♏	♈	♌	♑	♉	♎
OCT	♊	♎	♒	♋	♐	♈	♌	♑	♉	♎	♒	♊	♏
NOV	♌	♐	♈	♍	♑	♉	♎	♒	♋	♏	♈	♌	♑
DEC	♍	♑	♉	♎	♒	♋	♏	♈	♌	♐	♉	♍	♒

THE
SOLAR SYSTEM

THE STARS, OTHER THAN THE SUN, PLAY NO PART IN THE SCIENCE
OF ASTROLOGY. ASTROLOGERS USE ONLY THE BODIES IN THE
SOLAR SYSTEM, EXCLUDING THE EARTH, TO CALCULATE HOW OUR
LIVES AND PERSONALITIES CHANGE.

Pluto

Pluto takes 246 years to travel around
the Sun. It affects our unconscious
instincts and urges, gives us strength
in difficulty, and perhaps emphasizes
any inherent cruel streak.

Neptune

Neptune stays in each sign for 14
years. At best it makes us sensitive
and imaginative; at worst it
encourages deceit and carelessness,
making us worry.

Uranus

The influence of Uranus can make us
friendly, kind, eccentric, inventive,
and unpredictable.

Saturn

In ancient times, Saturn was the most
distant known planet. Its influence
can limit our ambition and make us
either overly cautious (but practical),
or reliable and self-disciplined.

SATURN

PLUTO

NEPTUNE

URANUS

Jupiter

Jupiter encourages expansion, optimism, generosity, and breadth of vision. It can, however, also make us wasteful, extravagant, and conceited.

Mars

Much associated with energy, anger, violence, selfishness, and a strong sex drive, Mars also encourages decisiveness and leadership.

JUPITER

EARTH

MARS

Earth

Every planet contributes to the environment of the Solar System, and a person born on Venus would no doubt be influenced by our own planet in some way.

The Moon

Although it is a satellite of the Earth, the Moon is known in astrology as a planet. It lies about 240,000 miles from the Earth and, astrologically, is second in importance to the Sun.

MERCURY

THE MOON

VENUS

The Sun

The Sun, the only star used by astrologers, influences the way we present ourselves to the world – our image or personality; the face we show to other people.

Venus

The planet of love and partnership, Venus can emphasize all our best personal qualities. It may also encourage us to be lazy, impractical, and too dependent on other people.

Mercury

The planet closest to the Sun affects our intellect. It can make us inquisitive, versatile, argumentative, perceptive, and clever, but maybe also inconsistent, cynical, and sarcastic.